THE WILDLIFE TREE

Written by Peter Emery

Illustrated by Deborah Emery

"Let nature be your teacher."
Peter Emery and Deborah Emery

The Wildlife Tree
Copyright © 2022 Peter Emery

ISBN: 978-1-63381-297-0

All rights reserved. No part of this book may be reproduced in any form or by any electronic or mechanical means, including information storage and retrieval systems, without permission in writing from the author, except by a reviewer, who may quote brief passages in review.

Illustrations by Deborah Emery

Designed and produced by:
Maine Authors Publishing
12 High Street, Thomaston, Maine
www.maineauthorspublishing.com

Printed in the United States of America

This book is dedicated to the children of our children, who, like our own three children, have explored the woods behind our home in Maine. We hope that our grandchildren will inspire others to appreciate the wonders in the woods, especially the Wildlife Trees.

Juliann, Enzo, Vera, Charlotte, Amelia, and Calvin

Many beautiful trees grow in the forests of Maine. They are alive with flowers, leaves, needles, nuts, seeds, and fruit.

Some trees in the forest are very different from these living trees. They no longer make leaves and their bark may be missing. Some people call them SNAGS. Others call them WILDLIFE TREES because so many animals use them for their homes!

Who is making the holes in the tree?

Who uses this big cavity at the base of the Wildlife Tree?

Who is peeking out from behind the Wildlife Tree?

The animal with the ringed tail and black mask is a RACCOON. Raccoons like to live in Wildlife Trees near a stream or pond.

They use their hands to search for crayfish under the water. Sometimes their hands can get them into trouble.

What animal has a bushy red tail?

What bird is gazing out of this hole in the tree?

A BLACK-CAPPED CHICKADEE is gazing out the opening of his nesting place. Chickadees talk to each other better than most other land animals. They can remember for many months where they stored their seeds and berries.

They often hang upside down on the underside of branches in search of insects. Hope they don't get dizzy!

What animal left all the "scat" at the base of the Wildlife Tree?

What is the animal with a cat-like face?

What baby bird is peeking his head out of the hole?

This hungry baby bird is an EASTERN BLUEBIRD. Bluebirds spend time together in small flocks eating grasshoppers, crickets, and beetles. Bluebirds get their name because of their beautiful blue feathers.

"I like to hover to look for insects on the ground."

What animal has the short tail?

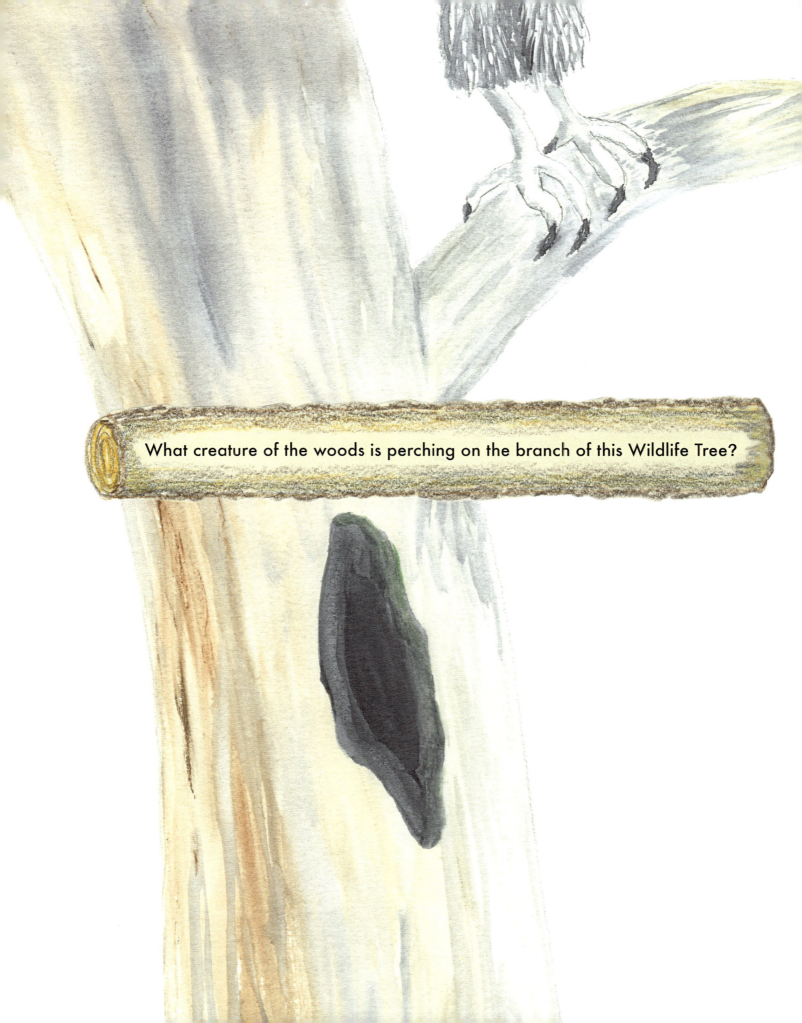

What creature of the woods is perching on the branch of this Wildlife Tree?

Wildlife Trees support the lives of many different animals. They provide food, shelter, and homes for nesting. Every forest needs Wildlife Trees!